CONTENTS

If you were able to stand on the moon,
you would see clouds floating
all around the planet Earth.

Clouds are important to Earth.
They bring it water
in the form of rain, hail, sleet, and snow.
They are part of the beauty
of nature.

Warm air rises
from the earth

Clouds are formed from warm air
that rises from the earth.
As the warm air rises, it cools,
changing into droplets of water or ice.
These droplets collect around
tiny bits of dust floating in the air.
As the drops mass together,
a cloud is formed.
When conditions are right,
rain, hail, sleet, or snow will fall.

Vapor turns to droplets in cold air and a cloud forms

Air starts to cool down as it rises over the mountains

Air is warm

Mountains often have clouds covering their peaks.

Most rain begins as ice.
High up in the clouds,
the water vapor freezes into ice crystals.
As the crystals grow bigger and heavier,
they fall through the cloud.
At the bottom of the cloud, the air is warmer,
and it melts the ice into water,
which falls as rain.
If the air at the bottom of the cloud is cold,
then the ice crystals do not melt,
and snow falls.

What is it like inside a cloud?
Just go outside on a foggy day.
Fog is really a cloud formed near the ground.

Dense, low cloud and fog can cause problems
for road traffic, sea traffic, and air traffic.

Clouds affect Earth's temperature.
Cloudy days are usually **cooler** than clear days.
This is because clouds bounce the sun's heat
back into space.

Cloudy nights are usually **warmer**
than clear nights.
This is because the clouds act like a blanket,
stopping Earth's warmth from escaping into space.

9

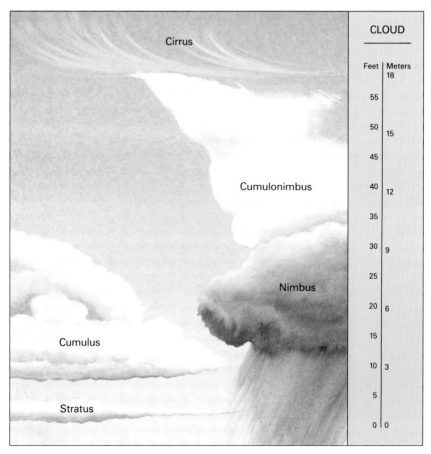

Scale indicates altitude in thousands of feet or thousands of meters.

There are many kinds of clouds.
Different clouds are seen at different heights
or altitudes above the earth.
Most clouds keep changing shape
because of the action of winds
and air movements high above the earth.

10

Strato means sheetlike.
Stratus clouds remind you
of a flat, gray sheet
stretched across the sky.
Drizzly rain or snow can fall
from this type of cloud.

11

Cumulus means heap or pile.
Cumulus clouds resemble
heaps of cotton
or mounds of whipped cream
billowing across the sky.
These clouds may grow to great heights.

When cumulus clouds are small,
they promise good weather.

When cumulus grow big,
there will be showers.

13

Nimbo means rain.
Dark, gray, rain-bearing clouds
are called nimbus clouds.
Better carry an umbrella
when you see these heavy-looking clouds
in the sky!

14

If you look out the window
during a thunder shower or hailstorm,
you will see mountainous clouds
with bulging bumps.
These are called *cumulonimbus* clouds.
Lightning comes from these clouds.
Tornadoes come from cumulonimbus clouds, too.

Cirro means a hair.
Cirrus clouds look like
curly, white tufts of hair
or lacy feathers.
Because cirrus clouds are formed
high in the atmosphere
where the air is cold,
they are made of ice crystals.
Cirrus clouds are so thin,
you can often see the stars through them
at night.

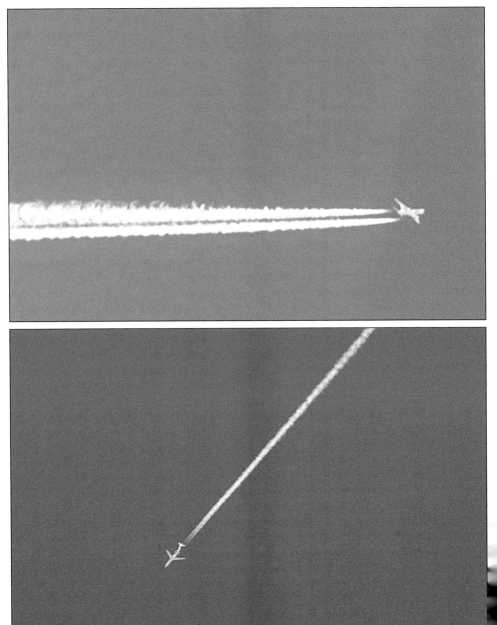

Have you ever seen the long,
white vapor trail left by a jet plane?
It shows that the plane is flying high
through very cold air.
That trail is formed in just the same way
as cirrus clouds.
Water vapor from the jet engines
is being frozen
into a cloud of ice crystals.

When you see cirrus clouds,
it usually means
that unsettled weather is coming.
You can also read the weather
when you watch a jet trail.
If the trail vanishes quickly,
good weather is coming.
If the trail stays in the sky
for a long time,
bad weather is on the way.

People have always told stories about clouds.
Long ago in ancient Greece,
people believed that the clouds
were the sun's cattle.

Over the years,
travelers and sailors have used clouds
to help them predict the weather.

Red clouds in the morning:
Sailors' warning.
Red clouds at night:
Sailors' delight.

When clouds at night are red, not gray,
It's safe to travel on your way.
If clouds at night are gray, not red,
Then rain will fall upon your head!

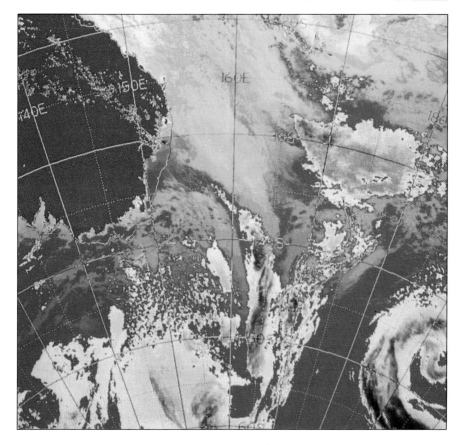

Nowadays, space satellites send back pictures
of Earth's clouds,
and weather forecasters use these
to make their daily weather forecasts.
They study clouds carefully.
Take a look at the sky today.
Do you know what the clouds are saying?

Clouds

INDEX